AF483530

CONTENTS

Andrew's Life

Andrew Mezen

Andrew's Life

Chapter 1: About Me

Hello, my name is Andrew Mezen. This book is about my life adventures and experiences. I am 30 years old. I am passionate about people. I love being around people. I am passionate about working with children. I love going to church on Sundays and serving at church. I love Jesus Christ. He is my personal Lord and Savior. I love roller coasters. My all time favorite game is Roller Coaster Tycoon and Planet Coaster. I love building amusement parks and riding all the rides you design. You get so creative with the game. My favorite color is red. I love to wear red sweatshirts, coats, and shoes. Red represents two major things they are the blood of Jesus and Republican. My favorite cereal is Honey Nut Cheerios and Apple Cinnamon Cheerios. I love video games. I play the Play Station 5. I grew up playing the Play Station 2. My all time favorite childhood game is Wheel of Fortune and Frogger for the Play Station. I would also enjoy games like Spyro and NBA 2k. Growing up I would love playing the Nintendo Wii. My favorite game is Wii Fit. I love playing it. I also love Super Mario games as well. My all time favorite game is Super Mario 64 for the Nintendo 64 and the Nintendo DS. My favorite sport is basketball. I played basketball since elementary school. I would play it at PE during my school years. I would play it in my backyard in El Segundo. I would play Horse with Dave and play it at school. When I was in grade school I loved PE. I loved running around the track in high school and running around the field in middle school. I love making new friends. I love talking to people. I am not able to drive. I am not able to raise Children on my own. My favorite food is spaghetti. Growing up I would always love to eat at Vince's Spaghetti house in Torrance, California. I would love when my mom made spaghetti. It was soo good. I would love to go to my Dad's house and eat Tayna's spaghetti. I love spaghetti. To this day I love ordering spaghetti from the different restaurants in our area. My all time favorite show to watch is Wheel of Fortune. I would play it on my PS2 and watch it on TV. I became really good at it. I even auditioned for the show a couple of times. My favorite soda is Dr Pepper. I also love Barq's Root Beer, Sprite, and Cherry Coke. When I was little I tried a sip of my mom's soda Diet Dr Pepper. I loved it ever since. My favorite candy is Sweet Tarts, Starbursts, and Fun Dips. My favorite fruit is strawberries. My favorite vegetable is Broccoli. My favorite subject in school is English. My favorite class was English 21 English Fundamentals. My favorite ice cream is Cookies N Cream. My favorite singer is Chris Tomlin. My favorite dessert is Pumpkin pie and Banana Pudding. My favorite holidays are Christmas and Thanksgiving. My favorite month is November. My favorite restaurant is Chipotle and Frankies. My favorite animal is a dog. My favorite music groups are Cedarmont Kids and Hillsong. My favorite amusement parks are Knott's Berry Farm and Six Flags Magic Mountain. My favorite movie is War Room. My favorite word is Relentless.

Why am I a Republican? I Back The Blue 100 percent. I support the Police. Every time I see a police officer I say Hi and Thank them for their service. I love this country. It breaks my heart to see what is happening all over this country and the world. I have been a Republican for all my life. I grew up with those values and they will never change.

I have traveled to all 6 continents. I still need to visit Australia. I have a passion for travel. I got it from my mom and grandparents. I have traveled around the world to several different exotic places. I have cruised to several different locations around the globe with my family. I have done several land trips as well with my family. I love traveling by airplane. I love the window and aisle seats. I love take off and landing. I have always loved air travel. It is so much fun. Long distance air travel is really hard though.

Here is a fun fact about me. Growing up I used to collect the movie stubs tickets. I used to separate them into movie ratings. It was really fun to seperate them all. I used to go to the movies a lot back in Los Angeles. My favorite movie genre is Disney animated. I enjoy kids movies. I used to enjoy comedy movies, but they have gotten out of control over the years. Ever since 2005 my family has put on Academy Award parties. We stopped a while ago though. We would have a theme and dress up for the show. Every year our family and friends came over for the party to enjoy the show. It was so much fun.

If someone were to ask me Andrew what makes you sad the most in this life? It would be families fighting with each other. It breaks my heart to see children fight with people/family members. I was taught from the moment I was a toddler that my sister is my best friend. Family should always get along. Sadly they don't always get along.

I love to socialize and meet new people. I love meeting new people at my job. I love going to church to learn more about Jesus Christ and make new friends. I am a social butterfly. I am not a shy person. I can walk up to anyone and introduce myself. I know I have to be careful who I talk to, but I talk to anyone who wants to talk.

I have a passion for buses and bus routes. I took the 232, 460, 6, 757, 3 and 7, 109, and many more in Los Angeles. I also loved the trains in Los Angeles. I loved the Greenline and the Red Line. I also loved the Gold Line that took me out to Azusa to visit my friend Zach. I remember in my speech I gave at the Generation NeXt farewell celebration I named all the bus and train routes to get to Six Flags Magic Mountain. I take the Greenline to the Silver or Blue Line. Next I take the Red

Line from the Metro Center to North Hollywood. Then I take the 757 Noho Express to the McBean transit center. From there I can either walk to the park or take the 3 or 7 to the park. It is about 3 in a half hours each way. I took the bus a couple times in Hickory. It was while I was living in my apartment.

Chapter 2: My Faith What Do I Believe

When I was born I was born blind. My doctors told my mom and dad I couldn't see. My mom and dad were very frightened. They went to our church and had a group of people pray over me. Over the years God healed my eyes. Over the course of my childhood and today I am able to see. It is a miracle. I wore glasses since 5th grade.

Growing up I loved going to church. I loved youth group. I loved summer camp at Bass Lake and Hume lake. I believe in Jesus Christ because he takes care of me and he loves me so much. He healed my blinded eyes when I was a child. I believe he is my ultimate healer, Protector, and Provider.

In middle school I became a Christian. I accepted Jesus Christ into my heart and got saved. I prayed a prayer like this: Dear Jesus Thank you for dying on the cross for me. Thank you for shedding your blood for me on the cross so I can have eternal life. Thank you for forgiving me of my sins. I am so sorry for the wrong things I have done. Please forgive me. I accept you into my heart. Please be my Lord and Savior. Thank you. In Jesus Name Amen! Surrender always comes before Salvation. The first step in becoming a Christian is Surrendering your life to Jesus Christ then accepting him into your heart and declaring him as Lord and Savior in your heart. What is the main purpose of being a

Christian? Being a Christian means to Love God and Love People, especially people who are hard to love. How do you love God. You love God by loving people. We love because Jesus Christ first loved us.

Who Is Jesus Christ? Jesus Christ is the King of Kings and the Lord of Lords. He is the son of God. He is the Father, Son, and Holy Spirit. He is the ultimate healer, provider, and protector. Jesus Christ is the creator of the universe. He i s my redeemer. Jesus Saves!!!! He created the world in 6 days and rested on the 7th day. He is the Prince of Peace. God's Grace is sufficient for me. God's Grace covers over me. I serve a big huge God that makes miracles happen everyday. He has done amazing things in my life and he can do amazing things in your life too. Jesus Christ is alive and performing miracles everyday. He is the wonder working miracle making God. God sees all! knows all! and Loves all!!! God's love is like a boomerang. You give it away and it comes back to you. I remember playing with a boomerang once. I throw it and it came back to me. God says to never worship Idols. What are idols? Idols are fake Gods. They get in your way of you fully worshipping God. It is something you put before your relationship with God.

So what are Christians supposed to do during our time here on earth? What is the great commission? "Therefore go and make disciples of all nations, baptizing them in the name of the Father and of the Son and of the Holy Spirit, and teaching them to obey everything I have commanded you. And surely I am with you always, to the very end of the age." Matthew 28:19-20 NIV

The Bible says to Honor your Father and Mother. "Honor your father and your mother, so that you may live long in the land the LORD your God is giving you" Exodus 20:12 NIV

I was born into this broken and fallen world filled with Sin. If the Bible says it is wrong to do something then it is wrong. The Bible refers to this as sin. We are all sinners. If people do things that are against God and his word it is sin. God's Word is sharper than any double-edged sword. It cuts to the core. God's Word is alive and powerful and can change any heart. I believe the book of Revelation is unfolding right in front of our eyes today. I believe we are living in the last days. I believe Jesus Christ is coming real soon. I do not know the day or the hour of his return but I am ready for his return for his church. I believe in the Pre-Tribulation Rapture. If I am still here during the 7 Year tribulation I will not bow down and worship the Beast and take the mark. If you ever are forced to take a mark on your hand or forehead REFUSE IT!!!!! The Mark of the Beast is a permanent mark and eternal consequences come if you take it and worship the Beast and his image Satan.

Choose wise friends. Choose friends who seek after Jesus Christ with their whole heart. Choose Friends who build each other up. It is so important to choose Christian friends that help each other out. I am not saying don't be friends with unbelievers. It is so important to share your faith with unbelievers so they can learn and come into a personal relationship with Jesus Christ and get saved. Be friends with them too. Just make sure they act appropriate and treat you well. We need friends by our side. I struggled making friends. To this day I struggle making friends. It is so important to connect to a Bible Believing Church. I recommend joining a small group Bible Study or a youth group. I remember the youth groups I was involved in growing up. My favorite was Uturn in El Segundo. Pastor Jon did an incredible job as the main youth pastor. I also thought Mario did an amazing job too as a youth leader. They changed my life. I made so wonderful friends.

My all time favorite saying is Devil You just got your butt kicked!!!! My God is Faithful!! My God is Powerful!!! and my God is in Charge!! You can't fire him and he will never retire!!! The devil is Satan himself all the way back in the Garden of Eden. I love that because everyday I am battling Satan the enemy. It is very easy to follow after Satan. It is easy to be involved in satanic things. Satan loves when you dwell in your past and doubts. Satan has messed with my life in the past. If you let Satan destroy your life he will. Just like if you let Jesus Christ control and be at the center of your life he will. If you invite him to live in your heart he will. It is easy to follow Satan, but it is very hard to follow Jesus Christ. Following Jesus is the best thing you can do. Jesus Christ is the ultimate healer, protector, healer, and rewarder. A personal relationship with Jesus Christ is the most important relationship you can ever have. The Bible says Broad is the road the leads to destruction and many will find it, but Narrow is the road that leads to Eternal Life and only a few find it. Many roads lead to destruction and so many people find them. There is only one road that leads to Eternal Life. That is through a personal relationship with Jesus Christ.

A question I hear a lot is if God is so loving how could evil exist in the world? The answer is Free Will. When God created us he gave us the will to choose right from wrong. People choose to do evil instead of Good. People turn their back on God. "If my people, who are called by my name, will humble themselves and pray and seek my face and turn from their wicked ways, then I will hear from heaven, and I will forgive their sin and will heal their land" 2 Chronicles 7:14 NIV

The Bible Says Jesus answered, "I am the way and the truth and the life. No one comes to the Father except through me" John 14:6 NIV

The Bible says if you seek after Jesus Christ with all your heart you will find him. "You will seek me and find me when you seek me with all your heart" Jeremiah 29:13 NIV. Seeking him is a daily thing. What does with all your heart mean? It means with everything you have. I can't just go to church on a Sunday. I can go and learn about God, but how does it impact your relationship with God. I remember from Hume Lake one of the pastors saying to us Knowing about God and Knowing God are two different things. You can know all about God, but still not have a personal relationship with him. It is kind of like do you know about Andrew Mezen or do you know Andrew Mezen because if you truly know me you would know. Going to church every Sunday does not make me a Christian. I became a Christian in middle school where I declared Jesus Christ as my Lord and Savior and I asked him into my Heart. The greatest commandment is Love your God with all heart, soul, mind, and strength, and the second is like it love your neighbor as yourself.

There is no greater love in the world than the love Jesus Christ has for you and me. Not one human being can love like how Jesus Christ loves us.

A life without Jesus Christ is a life filled with horror, anxiety, darkness, fear, sadness, and bitterness. Living life without Jesus Christ is dangerous and has eternal consequences. A life with Jesus Christ is a life filled with Joy, Peace, Contentment, and prosperity. A life without Jesus is a life that is wasted. If I have Jesus Christ in my life I have everything. If I don't have Jesus Christ in my life I have nothing.

How do people know I am a Christian? By this everyone will know you are a Christian by your love for one another. What is a Christian? A Christian is someone who follows Jesus Christ and has a personal relationship with Jesus Christ. Christian means Little Christ. A person has received Jesus Christ into their heart as their personal Lord and Savior. A Christian is commanded to show love and forgiveness no matter how hard it is. Reading your Bible. Going to Church. Singing Christian songs. Reading a devotional book are all important parts of being a Christian, but the most important part is how you treat the people around you. They will know us by our love to quote Aunt Mary. The Bible also says by their fruits you shall know them. The fruit of the spirit is love, joy, peace, patience, kindness, goodness, faithfulness, gentleness, and self control. When God refers to his church he means all Christians.

Yes we go to church on Sundays to worship God, but we are the church. The church isn't just a building the church is Christ followers Christians the body of Christ The Bride of Christ.

I remember several years ago my church Journey of Faith wrote a song called We Press On. They wrote it during the time I was struggling in high school. We press on towards the prize which is Jesus Christ. We won't give up. We won't give in. We press on. I would listen to it over and over again. To this day I still enjoy listening to it and thinking about how far I have come in my life. It is one of my favorite songs to listen to. I have it on my ipod.

I am not a perfect Christian. I am a sinner. I mess up. I make mistakes. What is sin? Sin is anything we say, think, or do that is against God and his Word the Bible. Sin separates us from God. There have been several times when I needed to forgive someone and needed forgiveness. Living the Christian life is the hardest thing to do. It takes perseverance and strength. Everyday I face challenges for which I am grateful because I know who is in control. God is in Control and he takes care of me.

In middle school and high school I overcame a lot of challenges. I was bullied by students and teachers. I liked a girl who didn't like me back. It hurt me really bad. She had mean friends. I believe Jesus Christ brought me through those storms. I loved every Thursday going to Christian Club Fellowship of Christian athletes and New Life Club. Mr. Sabosky was one of my favorite teachers I had in high school. He taught me so much about my faith while I was in school. I was in a few of his PE classes too. He was the leader of the Christian club on campus at El Segundo High School.

Another big miracle Jesus Christ did in my life was getting accepted into the Generation Next program in 2011. That program was a blessing from God. When I was in elementary school I got bumped up a grade. I was in 4th grade and I went up to 5th grade. If I haven't gotten bumped up a grade I would not had the opportunity for Generation Next. In Generation Next I lived near campus in an apartment with roommates. I learned how to cook, clean, take buses, manage money, make friends, and so much more. I still had challenges while in the program, but overall I had an awesome experience.

My faith has always been important to me. It is important for me to read my devotional book everyday and pray. I read my Bible too. My mom helps me understand the Bible better. I love reading my daily devotional book. It helps me understand the Bible more. I love listening to Christian music on my ipod. It can be very hard for me to share my faith with others. It can be very hard to share my faith with my family and friends. I do my best to share my faith with them. It is so important for Christians to share their faith so people can come into a personal relationship with God. I love going to church on Sundays and hearing the sermons. It helps me grow in my walk with Jesus Christ. Most importantly I grow in my daily quiet times. Sometimes I miss days, but I do my best to make sure to read and understand my devotional books.

In 2009 I got to go to Hume Lake Christian Camp with my church Journey of Faith. It was such an amazing experience. This was my first time away from home. I struggled alot, but I was able to make friends from my church and other churches at the camp. I was going though so much at school so being at camp really helped me with that. I also went in 2010 as well. I remember calling my mom on a couple collect calls with a payphone at Hume Lake. It costs about $50.00 dollars. In 2009 I went to Bass Lake with the Kenney family. Rosangela and Sean are the most amazing people I have ever met. They took me under their wing because I was away from home. William is one of my best friends. Evelyn, Amanda, and Julia are amazing as well. At Bass Lake I went wake boarding for the first time. It was really hard, but I was able to stand up. I also went tubbing off the back of the boat. It was so much fun.

At Hume Lake I enjoyed going on the blob. The Blob is a big blow up bouncer that you sit on one end and a person jumps and lands and you go flying up in the air. I loved all the morning chapel times. There were some powerful speakers there. I enjoyed all the fun rec times. I had so much fun at Hume Lake and Bass Lake.

One of my favorite verses in the Bible is "Put on the full armor of God so that you can take your stand against the devil's schemes For our struggle is not against flesh and blood, but against the rulers, against the authorities, against the powers of this dark world and against the spiritual forces of evil in the heavenly realms" Ephesians 6:11-12 NIV

I am always reminding myself of this one lifetime. This one lifetime I get to share my faith with others. This one lifetime I live life to the fullest. This one lifetime I bring Glory to God. This one lifetime I love everyone all around me. This one lifetime I show up for people and show them that I care about them. This one lifetime is all I have to live out my faith in Jesus Christ as a Christian. I should live everyday like it is my last day to live. Love like there is no tomorrow. Love people today because tomorrow is not promised. We are never guaranteed a tomorrow.

I look forward to the day I step foot into eternity Heaven. Heaven is a real place where all believers in Jesus Christ Christians go when they die. If you have accepted Jesus Christ as your personal Lord and Savior you go to Heaven when you die. Hell is a place where people go who reject Jesus Christ and his word the Bible and do not receive him as Lord and Savior in their hearts. Hell is a very scary place because that is where unbelievers go when they die. I remember Pastor Glen Martin from my old church saying "The Gates of Hell are locked from the inside" Hell is a real place. What is Hell? Hell is the place where you are eternally separated from God. It is judgement for unbelievers. There is eternal fire and gnashing of teeth. Never shake your fist in God's face. Shaking your fist in God's face has eternal consequences. The scariest words from Jesus Christ is depart from me I never knew you. One day all unbelievers will stand before the Great White Throne Judgement and be judged on how they lived on earth. A question I hear a lot is If God is so loving how could he send someone to Hell? Because he is a God of Justice. I believe the answer is Free Will. God does not want anyone to go to Hell. "The Lord is not slow in keeping his promise, as some understand slowness. Instead he is patient with you, not wanting anyone to perish, but everyone to come to repentance". 2 Peter 3:9 NIV

What is Repentance? Repenting means turning from your sin and turning to God for Forgiveness. Confessing your sin and saying sorry and turning from it to follow Jesus Christ.

If something isn't of God, then it is of Satan. It is so easy to get caught up with Satan. He goes around waiting for someone he can devour. He prowls around like a roaring lion looking to devour people. "Be alert and of sober mind. Your enemy the devil prowls around like a roaring lion looking for someone to devour". 1 Peter 5:8 NIV

We need generations of Christians who stand up for the truth and the truth only God's Word the Bible. We need generations and generations of Christians who hate to be lukewarm. We need generations of Christians who love each other. We need generations of Christians who hate laziness.

Please do not be a counterfeit Christian. A Christian who claims to follow Jesus Christ, but doesn't and who lives complete opposite of his word the Bible. It will break your parents heart if they raised you to believe and have a personal relationship with Jesus Christ and you completely turn your back on that and live a completely different immoral lifestyle.

Over these past several years God has shown up in my life in several ways. I have been a Christian for so long, but I feel that sometimes my faith isn't as strong as other days. I remember when I first went on medication and how I felt inside. I was really anxious. I remember being admitted to the hospital and being diagnosed with Bipolar. It was a really scary experience. I was really nervous about what was going to happen, but as I always say God is in control. He is Sovereign over me. There are several times that Satan has tried to come into my life and ruin it. I am reminded of this Bible verse Submit yourself To God. Resist the Devil and he will flee from you. I say Devil you've done it again!!!! You just got your butt kicked!!!! Satan has no power over my life. He can try to lie to me and make me feel terrible all he wants but he sure knows how to get his butt kicked.

A big question I have is if you knew you had one month left to live, how would you live? What would you do? Who would you tell your story to? The truth is none of us know when our time is up here on earth. I can't encourage you enough to make sure you are prepared for death. Death can occur at any moment. Make sure you are a Believer in Christ a Christian so you know for sure you are going to Heaven when you die. I do not know the day or time that I will die, but I know for sure I am going to Heaven to be with Jesus Christ forever. Death is a part of life.

Everyone of us has a story to tell. I encourage you all to share your story. Do not be shy. Share your story. Many people will listen and be encouraged by your story.

No one can go back and start a new beginning. Anyone can start today and make a new ending. If you want a fresh start in this life. If you want to become a Christian make today the day you put your faith and trust in him and trust him as your Lord and Savior of your life. Today is the day that the Lord has made. I will rejoice and be glad in it!!! Do not let your yesterdays affect you from today. The more you are prepared today the better you will be tomorrow.

One day I am going to stand before Jesus Christ on the Judgement Seat of Christ. I am going to give an account for the life I lived while on earth. He is going to place a crown on my head. I can't wait for that day he crowns me with rewards. He also will take rewards away as well. The Judgement seat of Christ is for all Christians who have trusted in Jesus Christ as their personal Lord and Savior.

3 |

Chapter 3: Early 2020

Wow 2020 has been a year for the books!! What made it so crazy? Well Lets dig in and discover so many lessons that this past year has taught us. In the beginning of 2020, I was hopeful for a great year. I enjoyed work and Special Olympics Swimming. I was making new friends and enjoying myself. I was going to movies and eating out and enjoying every day life.

Covid struck in the middle of March! What? Why? How? No one could understand what happened. Growing up my mom told me and my sister all about what was going to happen in the last days. I talked about some of the things in my past book about the Rapture and the 7 year Tribulation period. In this book I really dig into the roots of what I see and believe. I am not happy with what is happening all over the world. My heart hurts for the sick people. My heart hurts for the children in the world. I took myself off of social media for a period of time during the 2020 election because of how people were acting towards each other on social media. Social media is not the place for mean, inappropriate, unkind, comments/messages to one another. Social Media is the place for friends to connect with one another and to share our lives with. Over the years I have struggled making friends. I have made friends and thought they were my friends. I would call them fantasy friends. The saddest thing about social media is that it can tear people apart. It tore me apart in my last relationship. Embarrassment, shame, guilt, and pain came from it. I have a hard time accepting things. I have a hard time adding people who don't confirm my request. I have a hard time with so many aspects of social media. Social media has a negative affect on many people. Social media is bad in many ways. It brings out a lot of hurt feelings.

2020 has brought me so much tears, anxiety, stress, and fear. I am so glad I started on medication. It has been very tough for me to accept the fact of the new normal wearing masks out in public. Staying 6 feet away from people. Social Distancing! How on earth did we get here? I could not believe the results of the 2020 election. It just broke my heart to see what happened.

Since the start of Covid I had a picture in the back of my mind. I talked with my mom and thought about how could this tie into the end times. Over the course of the year many things took place that I can not even fathom could happen right before my eyes. Violence, horror, terror, Anger, rage, hatred, spread like wild fire all across the world. Why does this concern me? I am concerned mostly for children. I weep for the children in this world. Why? Because children are innocent little human beings. Children are not aware yet about the dangers and scary things of this world. Yes we as adults still teach them as best we can about things but if someone were to tell me that in 2020 I would have to wear a mask in public and stay 6 feet away from people and social distance. I would have laughed so hard. How could that happen?

I truly believe Covid was God's way of waking up the world. God uses broken people in this world to bring people to him. Life has been tough for so many years of my life. Yet 2020 was the most intense year in so many ways.

Despite the horror of 2020 a lot of awesome things happened in my life. I made a new friend. I got a new job at Bojangles. I loved my job at Bojangles. I made several new friends there. I enjoyed doing dishes and taking out trash. It was a great job. I learned a lot in 2020. I learned the importance of Faith. Even though I became a Christian many years ago I still could not believe what I saw on the internet and TV all over the world! Faith is not believing in things that I can see. Faith is not believing in worldly things like money and wealth. Faith to means believing in Jesus Christ and believing that he has given me eternal life through his son Jesus Christ. I believe that Faith requires action. Without Faith it is Impossible to please God. I believe Jesus Christ is not happy with the world today. Yet I still believe he loves each and every person. I believe he is still on his throne. I believe his time is near for his arrival for his church. I believe we could be living in the end times. I believe we are very close to the trumpet call the Rapture. Soon many many Christians living on this earth will quickly vanish into the air and meet Jesus Christ in the sky. The Bible talks about the Great Fallen away. Many Christians will turn cold. Many Christians will fall away from their faith.

Now is the time that we can not lose our faith in Jesus Christ. I am not saying we lose Salvation. I am saying that yes there are so many scary things in the world. Just because the world is out of control right now does not mean that my life needs to be out of control. Over the years my mom told me and my sister "You may be the only Bible someone gets to read" I thought about that so much over the years. I didn't really understand it. Going through 2020 and my challenging years in my life I am always reminded of how important my Faith in Jesus Christ is. The world is watching Christians today. Jesus Christ Sees all, Knows All, and Loves All!! He knows every heart. He hears every prayer. He is always in control. What is so interesting to me is all the talk about the election results and people saying things about what they think will happen and none of it has happened yet. Why? Because man is not in control. Only Jesus Christ is in control and only he has the power over the world. Satan is at constant work trying to deceive people and to scare people. Satan knows his days are short so he is working extra hard. Yet one day he will get his butt kicked and God will take him down and he will lose. Jesus Christ Always Wins!! Satan Loses!!! My all time favorite Awana Cubbies Bible life Lesson: You can never argue with God Jesus Christ. Why? Because he Wins Every time!!!!! My other one is Two Ears. One Mouth!!!! Listening is more important than talking!! Ask questions! Get to know people! The only way you get to know people is by asking questions. Take an interest in someone else's life.

I believe the problem is we are looking for answers in the wrong places. We go on the internet and get answers. We talk to people and get answers. We need to go to the root of what is really going on. We need to open up the Holy Bible God's Word and read it for ourselves. Going to church once a week for an hour isn't enough. Singing a few songs a few times a week isn't enough. We must take God's Word the Holy Bible and not just read it. We must take it and apply it to our life. We must instill the Word of God into our hearts. If it is not found in the Word of God the Bible then I want no part in it. Let me say that again if it is not in God's Word then I do not believe it. Knowing Jesus is the best thing in the whole world. I can not expect God to do his part if I do not do my part. Knowing About God is very different from Knowing God. My part is to Pray and seek Jesus daily. My Job as a Christian is to love everyone and share my faith with everyone! My job is to share my faith with the world. My job is not to point out each others sins Why? Because my sin is just as bad as your sin. We are all sinners. We are broken people. We are all in desperate need of a savior. Why are my beliefs so strong? Why did I choose to accept and follow Jesus Christ in 2005? Why do I believe what I believe? I believe what I believe because I have seen Jesus Christ work so many incredible miracles in my life from healing my eyes to getting accepted at Generation NeXt UCLA.

4

Chapter 4: Growing Up

When I was a little boy I wanted a sip of my mom's favorite drink Diet Dr Pepper. My mom told me no you won't like it. No its not good for you. Yet I pleaded and pleaded and I took a sip and now 30 years later Dr Pepper and Diet Dr Pepper are among my favorite drinks. I share that story because When I was little I did not understand a lot of things. I did not truly know where I found my identity. I did not really know who my true friends were. I did not really understand the Bible. Growing up with a disability I had a lot of questions and things that I did not like.

Today the world is filled with darkness. The world is turned upside down. The world is spinning out of control. The world seems so big and I seem so small. Yet I believe with all my heart that Jesus Christ is still the King of Kings and Lord of Lords.

Growing up I was part of a special needs organization called Casa Colina. I went to Haliburton Forest 3 hours outside of Toronto, Canada. I went snow shoeing, dog sledding, and snow mobileing. There was a group of us that went. I went with my mom. This was back in 2007 when I was in 8th grade. I also participated in their Land meets sea sports camp for a couple years. I did several different activities. I did deep sea fishing, jet skiing, and much more. I was so grateful for this opportunity. When we left Canada there was a 100 degree difference in temperature. We went from 50 below to 80 degrees back in Los Angeles,

California. I really miss that program. I had such a great time making friends and participating in all the activities they had for us.

Growing up my mom would take me and my sister to really delicious restaurants. There was a season where we would go to Mimi's Cafe. I remember I would order the pot roast and eggs. They had really good lemonade. We would go to Wahoo's Fish Tacos and I would order the teriyaki steak bowl. It was soo good. She would take us to Rubios Fish Tacos too. We ate there a lot during a summer. We would go to the mall on Friday nights and eat at Mongolian BBQ. I remember my mom would take me and my sister to the AMC theaters several times. We would get Wetzel Pretzels. I remember I loved Nestle Strawberry Milk. I would get that when we went to the movies. I would love to get popcorn too. I would share drinks with my mom and sister.

Over the years as I am getting older I am figuring out that it doesn't matter what church I go to as long as they believe what I believe. I doesn't matter what my favorite Church songs are. It doesn't matter my experience at church. What truly matters is what my entire faith is dependent on. What matters is the fact that Jesus Christ was crucified on the cross 2 thousand years ago. He was beaten, tortured, mocked, spat on, laughed at, and he died. Why? Because he loves us. He died to take the punishment for my sins and yours. He didn't just die. He rose again 3 days later and made a way for us to go to Heaven. God gave his one and only son Jesus Christ to save us. Why Because he loves us. The world started with God. The world ends with God. Life began with Jesus Christ. The world will end with Jesus Christ. The greatest gift I ever received was the Gift of Salvation. Salvation is only a gift that Jesus Christ can give. Only Jesus Christ is the way to Heaven. There is no other way. The only way is through the cross.

So why do I not believe everything I read on the internet? Why did I delete my social media account for a period of time? Because my identity is not found on the internet. My identity is not found in other people. My identity is not found in my bank accounts. My identity is found in Jesus Christ and him alone. Jesus Christ the creator of the universe created me so special and when he looks at me he doesn't see sin he sees a masterpiece. Why? Because when he was on the cross he had me on his mind. He has a purpose and plan for my entire life. He washed my sins away in his blood.

"For God so loved the world that he gave his one and only Son, that whoever believes in him shall not perish but have eternal life" John 3:16 NIV

Over the years I dealt with a lot of different emotions. I had a lot of questions I did not truly know the answer to. I struggled with so many different things. I was upset at things I couldn't do and things I wanted. I wanted to raise children and my mom told me no. I wanted to drive and my mom told me no. I wanted to graduate from college and I didn't make it. Why because those aren't God's plans for me. See when I was younger I was diagnosed with an Intellectual Disability. I was told in school that I had learning challenges. I was told in school that I can not graduate from high school like everyone else. I was told that I can not learn like everyone else. It was very hard for me to accept those things. Growing up I struggled with anger. I was very angry in high school. Why? Because I was in a small special day class where I was bullied by other students. I struggled with friendships with my peers. I had tough teachers who picked on me at times. Yet I felt very alone and scared as a student. Why? Because I didn't truly know my identity yet.

Over the years I am learning more and more that I was created by God with a purpose. When Jesus Christ was on the cross he had me in mind. He created me in my mom's womb. I am fearfully and wonderfully made. God created me because he knew I have the strength to live this life. I am forever grateful for my personal relationship with Jesus Christ.

During my senior year in high school I got accepted into the UCLA Generation NeXt program. Here is the story. When I was in fourth grade I got bumped up a year. So I went from 4th to 5th grade. I skipped a grade. I was very nervous to go into middle school at such a young age. The UCLA program was a one year transition program for young adults with Intellectual Disabilities. It was from 2011-2012. If I hadn't gotten bumped up a grade in school I wouldn't had gotten the opportunity to attend this one year transition program at UCLA. 2011-2012 was a year filled with adventure and challenges. I learned so many different things. I learned to manage money. I learned public transportation. I learned how to interact with peers. I made friends. I learned how to live independently. I learned how to get to my favorite amusement park in Los Angeles, California. Generation Next was such a gift from God. I learned and grew so much from that program.

Chapter 5: What Is An Intellectual Disability

What is an Intellectual Disability? When I was little, I was diagnosed with an Intellectual Disability at age 4. What is that? An intellectual disability is like a learning disability. It affects school, work, and home life. When I was younger I struggled to use the bathroom at night. This was very challenging for me. I learn differently then my peers. I still learn but at a slower pace and at a lower ability academic level. Over the years I have struggled with this. I have had many doubts in my life. I have dealt with so many obstacles in my life when I was in grade school. I struggled a lot with academics. I could hardly read. I had friends but very few. I was in Adaptive PE. Adaptive PE is a group of special needs students playing sports together.

Growing up in grade school I was having a very hard time with academics. As an adult I see why I was struggling so much. I have learned that if the academic level is passed 5th grade that I will have a very hard time learning and comprehending it. For example if you put a book or math problem in front of me that is at a high school or college, or even middle school level I can not understand it. I am able to learn academics at an elementary school level.

That is why my mom spoke so candid to me. She had to repeat so many things to me over the years so I could understand them. My mom told me things like Andrew you can not raise children. Andrew you can not drive. Andrew you won't be able to graduate high school with a diploma or college with a degree. I was heartbroken. I believe in my heart that my mom could be wrong at times. Driving is scary anyway so no I do not feel comfortable driving. That is why I take the bus or walk. I love walking. It is the best exercise you can do. I love listening to music while I walk especially where I live.

As an adult I am buying books that are at my level. My level is between 2nd grade through 5th grade. I listen to songs that are at my level. I play video games that are at my level.

When I was younger I asked a lot of questions. I was like Why Me? How can this happen to me? I didn't understand yet my disability and how it affected me. As I got older I started to understand a lot more about God and how he created me. He created me with a purpose. His plans are much bigger and better than my plans. I love to say Mom knows Best! Jesus Christ Knows Better!!! As an adult I still try to wonder why sometimes. The biggest one is raising Children. Raising kids was always something I wanted to do, but because of my disability I am unable to take care of a child. I am very sad about it, but I am so happy I get to serve at church in Children's ministry and get to love and teach children.

Growing up I accomplished a lot of things. I remember at my high school senior awards night I was called to the stage and received a Character Growth Scholarship award. I went through a lot during my childhood, but I am the person I am today because of it. Today I don't look at my life and say I am intellectually disabled. I say I have learning challenges. I still am disabled which I put in the back of my head, but it does not stop me from living life to the fullest. I know I have strength and weaknesses, but I overcome them. I am so grateful for the challenges in this life because I become a stronger person because of them. I work very hard at trying my best to be very independent. I remember when I lived in Los Angeles I would take buses and trains all around town. In North Carolina I make sure to stay active and work.

I have big dreams. I want to get married one day. I want to raise a family even though I cant. I want to get a job on a cruise ship. We all have dreams. We all have things in this world we want to accomplish. Children have big dreams too. I want to live on my own or with my future spouse. The Bible says Delight in the Lord and he will give the desires of your heart. I have been praying for years for things. I have been blown away by how God has worked in my life. I just have to believe in myself and keep on praying. God is a God of Miracles.

6 |

Chapter 6: School Years

Growing up I always loved going to school. In elementary school I would love to go on the swings. I would love to do Graphic Arts where you use color pencils to figure out what the mystery picture is. I would always enjoy walking to school to learn new things. I would enjoy meeting new friends and going on awesome field trips like the Queen Mary and to the Manhattan Beach Pier. I loved elementary school.

When I got to middle school I began to struggle. I struggled with maturity. I struggled making friends. I was in a special day class. Even though I loved PE I struggled in that class too. I was very young for my age. I remember my horrible art class in the 7th grade. My teacher was really awful. She didn't treat me well as a student. She took away my yearbook at the end of the trimester and gave me a bad grade. Thankfully I got it back. My PE teacher was good even though she was tough on me. My Special needs class teacher was great even though she was tough on me too.

When I got to high school I struggled severally. I was in a basic skills class 4 periods a day. It was fun because we cooked on Fridays. We would go out into the community during the week. I enjoyed going to the library even though I wasn't a big reader. We would go to the grocery store to pick out what we were making that week. It was also very hard too. It was really hard because I was still very immature. I liked a girl but she didn't like me back. Her friends were not nice. I got myself into trouble a handful of times because of this girl. I took some awesome classes in high school despite my challenges. I loved PE, Sculpture/Ceramics, Financial literacy/Business Math, Graphic Arts, and photography. Despite my challenges I still enjoyed school. I loved Christian club on campus on Thursdays. I loved weight training class. I met some great friends in high school. Even though for some of them we have gone our separate ways. I still remember them. My best friend from Childhood is Ian Baxter. We still are in touch. We visit each other sometimes. He moved away and I moved away, but we remain best friends.

What are Bullies? Bullies are people who go out of there way to pick on other people. They make fun of people and laugh at people. They can do a lot of other things. I have seen bullies all throughout my life not just in school. Bullies are sad people. Bullying is never ok and should never be tolerated. When I say I have been bullied by teachers I mean I have been treated unfairly by teachers sometimes. I still was very immature in high school. There were students in my class who bullied me. Bullying is a big cause in suicide. Students can come home from school or wherever and can do self harm because of bullies. Never be a bully. If you see a bully hurt someone go and help that person and tell a responsible adult right away.

I had some great teachers over the years. I also had unfair teachers. When I say unfair teachers I mean teachers who treated me unfairly. Teachers if you are not liked by your students then I recommend evaluating how you treat them. If students don't want to come to school and learn then that is really bad because school should be a safe place for children and teens to come and learn. Teachers should have a passion for teaching. I know teaching is hard. I remember my Child Development professor saying "parenting is hard, being a teacher is harder" Teachers believe in your students. Teach them and watch them learn and grow. The more you put into your teaching the more you and your students will get out of it.

There were days I didn't want to come to school. I remember one day my class went to the library and I went into the elevator. The substitute teacher yelled at me so loud in the library and I started to cry. That Friday when I got home I said I didn't feel comfortable coming back to school. Another time I remember my choir teacher from high school wanting to fail me because I didn't complete a required project. Another time my art teacher from middle school took away my yearbook and gave me a bad grade. She was an unfair teacher. Still I enjoyed going to school despite the bad things my teachers had done.

Teachers sometimes you will have special needs students in your classroom. It is important to understand the needs of your students whether they have special needs or not. Going to school with special needs is extremely hard. Teaching is hard work. Even though all my experience is with young children I still can see how hard it is being a teacher.

Children and students respect your teachers!! Your teachers are there to help you learn and become better students. They give there time and efforts to create a learning environment for you. I understand that some teachers may not like every student, that is how it was when I was in school, but do the best you can. If you walk into school and do as your told and be respectful you will succeed and go far in life. If you have a hard time respecting your teachers, you will have a very hard respecting your Managers when you get to the workplace.

I am always amazed to this day how Jesus Christ works in my life. Several years ago I would have never dreamed of moving away from home. Living on my own, taking public transportation, having a job, managing money were only a dream for me. Looking ahead to 2021 and all the years leading up to it I am so amazed at what God can do in the midst of the storms and vallies and trials in life.

One of the biggest things in my life was moving away from El Segundo up to UCLA in Westwood. In 2011 after I graduated high school I got accepted into a one year transition program at UCLA called Generation Next. It is so crazy to believe that God provided a way for me to be a part of the one year transition program. When I was in 4th grade I got bumped up to 5th grade. If that did not happen I would not have gotten this once in a life time opportunity to attend this year one transition program at UCLA.

In September of 2011 my mom helped me move up to UCLA for the one year Generation NeXt program. I was really sad to leave home, but excited too. At UCLA I had a roommate. His name is Martin. He was a special friend during my time at UCLA. We were buddies. I met some awesome girls in the program as well. Some of them were mean to me though. I learned so much. I learned how to cook. I learned how to take the bus. I learned how to manage money. I learned about what it is like having a job even though I didn't work when I was there. I joined UCLA's Campus Crusade for Christ group. I went up to the mountains with them a few times and had so much fun. I came home a lot too because I felt homesick. Generation Next was a huge blessing in my life. Despite its challenges it was an amazing program and an amazing learning opportunity. I thank God everyday for such a great learning experience there. I miss it, but I still remain in contact with a few of the friends I made there.

After the program I continued on my educational journey to West Los Angeles College. West Los Angeles College provided me with great learning opportunities and challenges. I have never In a million years have even dreamt of attending a community college with regular students. It was one of my greatest accomplishments I have experienced. I got to try out several different classes. I got to experience some different classes in different fields. Some I could do and some I could not do. I took a couple Hospitality and travel classes. They were really fun, but they were online. Online classes were really challenging and not my favorite classes. I was part of the Disabled Programs and services. I had an awesome counselor named Nancy. Betty was in charge and she was very helpful too. I was able to get accommodations such as extra time on tests, a note taker, and help with my classes. I loved the services. They were very helpful.

In the Spring of 2014 I was so excited to take Child Development classes. I loved learning about children. Not only did I enjoy learning about children I also got to work with children at my church. I got to serve in Awana Cubbies and Sparks. It was such an amazing opportunity. I enjoyed every week taking the bus down to Journey of Faith and serving in Awana. That is where I grew in my faith. Giving back to my community has been such a great opportunity for me. The biggest thing I learned when working with children is to constantly show up for them. Show them that you care. They look up to us as adults. Being a role model for them is so important.

I loved my English classes. I started out in English 21 English Fundamentals. I had an incredibly passionate professor who helped me out in her class. I passed that class with a B. It was challenging in ways. The next class I took was English 28 Intermediate Reading and Composition. My favorite professor only taught it during winter session at that time. I met an amazing friend named Siddiga. She put together a study group for the students in the class. I was able to pass the class with an A. I was so proud of myself because there was lots of reading and writing in the 5 week winter session class. After the winter session I really wanted to try English 101 College Reading and Composition. My favorite professor only taught it for the 8 week spring semester and 5 week winter session. I attempted it but did not finish the class. I dropped it early on. The reason is I can not understand reading material at a college level. My brain can only comprehend at a elementary school level. I think my writing ability is how I passed all the other English classes. I was really sad because I really wanted to pass English 101 but I couldn't do it at all. I was proud I made it that far.

I loved my time at West Los Angeles College. In 2015 I started taking classes at Los Angeles Trade Tech College. I would take the Green and Blue Line train to get there from El Segundo. I took more Child Development classes. I took a Child Health and Safety class and a Child Curriculum class. I was in the middle of a Child Development class when I got hit by the car and had to drop my class. I was really bummed. I loved eating in the college's cafeteria. There food was really good. I loved LA Trade Tech College. I am so glad I spent time there.

Overall despite the classes I dropped I had an amazing time taking classes. I remember in 2018 I took a water aerobics class at West LA College. I made several new friends. It was really fun. My favorite classes were English and Child Development. I had incredible passionate professors for all my classes.

Taking these classes has shown me what I am capable of. In grade school I really didn't know what I was capable of. I am so proud of my accomplishments over the years. Taking classes at a community college was a huge highlight for me. I loved all of them and learned so much from them. I had excellent professors who really taught well. I miss those days of taking the bus to school and eating in the cafeteria. I can't believe I am 30 now. I am really glad I took Hospitality and Travel classes. Even though they were online I learned so much from them.

When it comes to making friends we have to be so careful who we choose to be our friends. It is so important to be kind to everybody. It is so easy to make friends who are bad influences on us. Friends can make or break us. They can tell us things that our parents would not like us to hear. They can lead us in the wrong directions and if we are not careful we can get ourselves in big trouble. When choosing the right friends make sure they treat you well and that they act appropriate. I have had several friends who I thought were my friends but they were not my friends. They were my Fantasy Friends. Choose your friends wisely. Make wise decisions when it comes to making friends. If you are not sure ask your parents or a responsible adult about it. It is so hard to make friends because we don't know how they will impact our lives. If you see somebody sitting alone at the dining hall go and sit with them. If you see someone struggling in class help them out. Be the change you wish to see in the world. It only takes one person to change someone's life and you can be that person. So go beyond yourself and make an impact in the world today because in this world we need God and we need each other. The greater you make the person next to you, the Greater you will be. We need those friends who walk beside us through thick and thin. I sure wish I had people by myside when I was in grade school. I had youth group but that was later in school. It is really sad there is a lot of bullying in schools. If you encounter someone being bullied please go and help that person out right away. Make sure they are ok. We live in a very sad and broken world where social media and cell phones are at our fingertips and they are destroying our youth. Social media has a really negative impact on your youth of today. We have to be so careful on it. I have gotten hurt on it several times.

It is easy hanging out with friends that are easy to love and get along with. It's easy to hang out with my best friends. It is hard to hang out with difficult people. Jesus Christ commands us to love people who are different from us. He commands us to love the unlovable. He commands us to love everybody even if they are hard to be around.

Chapter 7: Family Trips

Growing up my Grandparents would take the family on cruises. I would always enjoy them. We would go to Mexico, Caribbean, Hawaii, Alaska, and Europe. I would always enjoy the elevator on the cruise ships. When I was younger I was obsessed with elevators. I would love to ride up and down on them. I remember a time on a cruise when I got in the elevator and an elderly lady was on it. She said "every time I get on this elevator that little boy is on here". On cruise ships me and my cousins would love to join the children's group. It had a lot of different names. On Holland America it was Club Hal. I remember on the first Europe cruise we all made tye dye t shirts. I always enjoy the dining room on cruise ships. I love to try the different foods. I would love to eat steak on the cruise ships. I would really enjoy the different ports of call. Hawaii was a fun cruise. They had really fun activities. My favorite activity on cruise ships is playing Trivia. I love joining groups and playing together. I would have such a great time with my cousins Connor and Collin Obryan. We would go tour the ship. We would enjoy eating in the dining room. We would love the activities they had for kids on the ship. I also loved touring the ports with them as well. I miss those days where my family would come together and travel the world on a cruise ship to many different ports of call.

My first ever river rafting trip was down a river in Yellowstone. It was a class 3 half day river experience. It was my first time river rafting. I loved it so much I started going down a lot more rivers. In 2011 my mom took me down the Middle Fork of the Salmon river in Idaho. It was a week long river journey with class 3 and 4 whitewater. My sister loves river rafting too. We also like tubbing down rivers too. White water rafting is one of my all time favorite outdoor activities I love to do. A few hours away from my home in Hickory is Deep Creek. It is a fast flowing tubbing whitewater river. Its like class 2 white water. It is very easy to flip on that river. Thankfully I haven't flipped on the bigger whitewater rivers.

Growing up me, my mom, my sister, Dave and Matt and Sean took a road trip to Yellowstone. We would stop in Primm Nevada on the way to ride Desperado the roller coaster at the state line. I would really enjoy it. In Yellowstone we would saw Geysers and wild animals. I remember I was putting on my shoes in the back of the car and a herd of buffalo crossed in front of me. We loved to see all the wild buffalo. I remember they would come so close to your car its like you can lean out an touch them, but you can't.

In 2012 my mom took me and my sister on a road on the east coast. This was long before we moved here. We started in Fort Worth Texas, and drove all the down to the Florida Keys. We put 4,000 99 miles on the rental car. We went to Six Flags over Texas a couple of times. It was really fun, but it was so hot I got dehydrated. We went river rafting down Deep Creek in North Carolina. That was really fun. I remember I got a major headache and was super hungry. We stayed at a haunted hotel called Balsam Mountain Inn at that time. That was a really special trip. I had so much fun with my family.

One of my favorite trips I went on was to South Africa in 2013 with my mom and sister. We did an incredible game drive where we saw the big 5 Leopard, Lion, Elephant, Rhino, and Cape Buffalo. There was a disturbing scene where 2 male lions took down a giraffe. We didn't see it happen but we saw footage of the aftermath of it. We saw a lot of animals that trip. We saw Victoria Falls in Zimbabwe. We took a microlight flight over the falls. It was really neat. That was such a special trip. I loved it so much.

Growing up Dad and Tayna would take me and my sister to Mammoth Mountain in California. That is where I first learned how to snowboard. It was such a fun time. I would go for several years with them. I would join disabled sports in Mammoth so I got help with snowboarding.

In 2019 my family rafted the Grand Canyon. We did a 7 day motor raft down the river. It was really hot on the trip. We had an excellent time rafting the Grand Canyon. I remember I would love to sit in the front of the raft when it was safe to do so and get drenched by the rapids. I remember at the end of the trip the last day we got of the raft and was greeted with Subway sandwiches and soda. That was a really memorable trip.

In February of 2022 me, my mom, and my Grandpa took a cruise down to Antarctica. We had such an amazing time. We saw lots of penguins, glaciers, and icebergs. We sailed on the Sea Spirit. We got big red parkas to wear in the cold. This was towards the end of Covid, but Covid was still going on. They did lots of testing before you got on the ship and while you were on the ship. We met some amazing friends named Darold and Laura, and Kim and Ken. We all sat together for our meals at the dining room. The food was excellent. The trip was just magical. I got a new sweatshirt of Antarctica with patches on it that I wear in the winter. There were a few disappointments. We didn't get to do the polar plunge or sleep on a glacier. Overall it was an amazing trip that we will never forget.

In January of 2023 me, my mom, my stepdad, and grandpa did a cruise in Africa. It was so much fun. There were several days at sea. We sailed onboard Oceania Nautica. It was such a nice ship. We did a pre cruise safari. It was incredible to see all the animals. There was really good food on the ship. I ate spaghetti a lot. We met some great friends Larry and Ben while playing Trivia. We played trivia several times. Sadly halfway through the trip my Grandpa became ill. He came down with pneumonia. We had to disembark the ship in the Seychelles. Grandpa got admitted to the hospital. He was there for a few days as he recovered. He was a trooper. We then were able to fly home back to North Carolina.

In April of 2024 my mom took me and my sister to the Caribbean on a cruise. We went to several different ports. My favorite was Aruba! We had such a fun time. We loved touring the ship. We loved eating at the dining room for dinners. I got spaghetti, steak, and fish. I had good omelets too. We had the soda pass so I got coke and sprite to drink. We were on the Norwegian Sky. It was a really nice ship.

On May 25th 2024 me my mom, my grandpa, and stepdad went on a 7 day cruise on the Great Lakes. We took my Grandpa for his 90th birthday. We had an amazing time. We went to awesome ports of call. We met some amazing friends on the ship. We saw Niagara Falls. It was my Grandpa's first time seeing Niagara Falls. The cruise ship had an amazing food. I got steak, pasta, and pizza. They had a Cold Stones type ice cream stand. I also loved the Gelato ice cream with Oreos. We ate in the World Cafe almost every night. It was delicious. They had a really cool pool/hot tub jacuzee. They had different rooms where you can go into such as a steam room, a Sana, and an ice cold bucket room. Their pool was really nice. I got a haircut onboard for the first time on a cruise ship. The ship had superior staff onboard. They went above and beyond for us. We enjoyed getting served from Fany, Ralph, and Soley. They did an amazing job making us happy. The employees seemed very happy to be there. Our room Stewarts did an incredible job as well. It was great to see Grandpa have a great time. We really enjoyed ourselves. It was mine and Grandpa's first time on Viking. It was so cool because we were on an expedition ship. The ship had 350 passengers. There were a few tender ports. The trip went by fast, but It was so worth it.

I love to travel on airplanes. I love walking through the airport and finding our gate. I love arriving at the airport. My favorite part of flying is taking off and landing. I have been on several flights over the years. Flying is really fun. Flying can be very challenging if you travel long distances.

I am forever grateful for the trips I have been on with my family. I am thankful for the experiences I had with my family. Traveling is a huge part of my life and I am forever grateful to be able to travel the world. I am so grateful for my parents and grandparents who instilled in my a love for travel and have taken me and my sister on so many wonderful trips around the world.

8 |

Chapter 8: The Jenna Years
2016-2018

One ordinary summer day in 2016 I met this woman on a special needs dating website. Her name is Jenna. Jenna and I had similar needs and interests. She and I lived in two different states. She seemed like a very good match.

Two challenged adults in different states how is this ever going to work? Well in my heart I really wanted it to work. We talked on the phone and our parents talked as well. The relationship started in the summer of 2016. In spring of 2017 I flew up there to visit her. She lived in Idaho. She was very sweet and her family was nice. It was very hard to figure out if she was the one. The weekend was exciting yet challenging in ways. I was nice to stay at her grandparents house. When I flew back home I was having thoughts like is she really the one?

Over the next several months and couple years we stayed together I struggled alot with the relationship/friendship. I was confused whether or not she truly loved me. Wether or not I was doing the right thing.

See I knew in my heart something was wrong in this relationship. First of all she lived far away. Second her step dad didn't treat me well. He deleted me on social media and blamed that the website deletes people. Her brother treated me bad as well not as bad as the step dad though. She had a nice family. Her grandparents were great and her sister was very nice as well. Her mom welcomed me as well. It was still very hard to know what to do. I enjoyed getting to know her over the course of the couple years we were together. I enjoyed her family. The distance was very hard. It was hard to be away from her. Her cousins we great too. We all went to a local amusement park near where her cousins lived.

The winter of 2018 I went out there and spent a month with her family and things just went downhill. Her step dad wasn't nice. Her brother wasn't nice to me either. Jenna was still very nice as she knows how to be. I knew in my heart something was really wrong. She came and visited me in California in the summer of 2018. After her visit the relationship came to an end and things got ugly. It was an ugly breakup that I never want to go through again. I broke up with her. I knew a lot of things inside that I just was very concerned about. She and I had a good relationship together, but I was very concerned at a lot of things. It destroyed me to break up with her, but I knew it was for the best. Long distance relationship are hard and most of the time do not work. Never break up over the phone and texts. Always go straight to the person and talk to them. Even if the relationship is long distance still you should talk to them. You should always have face to face conversations especially if you are breaking up with the person.

What I have learned through this relationship is to never force anything. I felt with this relationship it was very forced because the distance was really hard. It is best to take it slow and get to know each other before making any big decisions. Meeting online wasn't the best idea for me. It is best to meet people who live in your area. Long distance relationships are very hard and most of the time do not work. I really want a partner. I want to get married one day. Finding a partner is really hard especially for people with disabilities.

9

Chapter 9: My Grandma Shirley Durtschi

Shirley my grandma was the most unique special, authentic woman I have ever known in my lifetime. She truly was a such a role model in so many ways. Even though she had her struggles as did I she taught her family so many wonderful and tough life lessons. She taught me how to treat people. She taught me how to love Jesus Christ and act like him. She taught me how to love my family. My Grandma did so much for me and my sister. Every Sunday her and my grandpa Arnold Durtschi took me, my sister, and my mom out to lunch. Every Sunday after church I wrapped my arms around my grandma. Every Sunday we all would go out to restaurants and eat great food. My favorites were Big Wok and Vinces. During the week we would meet them at a restaurant near their house. This was a weekly tradition.

Today as my family continues to live on. I am always reminded of the legacy Shirley left behind as she passed away in April of 2018. She will always be remembered and never forgotten. She spent many years struggling. I spent many many years loving her and being the best Grandson I can be.

I honestly believe if my grandma were to walk the earth today she would be outraged about what's happening all across the world and especially in our country. My Grandma loved her country. My Grandma loved the 4th of July. That was her holiday.

My grandma was a very special woman. She adored her family. She adored her children my mom and my aunt. She loved me through all my times of trials and loved me every second of everyday. My Grandma had issues like me and you. She was faithful to the finish line. She taught her family so much. She was constantly there to chat and to talk about life and all the problems life brought. She gave me hugs every time after church and after lunch. I loved every year going up to Big Bear with the family. I adored my grandma. To this day I believe she would have been outraged at what is going on in the world today. She was a tough woman. She was bold and she was a family woman and a Christian. She loved this country. She loved the 4th of July. She took her family on amazing cruises. She passed away in April of 2018.

My Grandpa Arnold Durtschi is still alive and living with us. He is 90 years old. He loves spending time with the family and loves watching TV. I love going out to eat with him. He loves Mexican food. He loves hikes with the family and he loves his daily walk. He is such a joy to have around. We get to enjoy him and he is a blessing to us. His favorite word is Folks. Alright Folks he says!!

I am forever grateful for my grandparents. They have taught me so much. They have loved me so much. I can't believe my Grandma has been gone for several years now. She was a Warrior. I am grateful I still can enjoy my Grandpa. I miss my grandma so much, but I am looking forward to the day I see her in Heaven when I die.

It's to late for my Grandma, but it is not too late for anyone of us who are alive. My Grandma taught me what it is like to love family and love Jesus. I am constantly reminded that my life can be snatched away in a second and to constantly be grateful for every opportunity. Family is extremely important. Most of all is a personal relationship with Jesus Christ. Grandma has shown us in many ways what a personal relationship with Jesus Christ is like. She has demonstrated her love for her family and for Jesus. Every time I think of her I am reminded of the important things in life.

Grandma everyday I miss you. Every day I think about you. If you were to walk the face of the earth today I know deep down how you would feel. I can't wait till that day I get to see you in Heaven and wrap my arms around you. Thank you for being the best caring and loving grandma. I love and miss you!!!

10 |

Chapter 10: Moving To North Carolina

In 2019 my family moved across the country. Me, my Mom, Grandpa, and Stepdad are moving out to Hickory, North Carolina. My dad is back in Los Angeles, California. For me preparing to move across the country was extremely hard especially moving from Los Angeles. It was hard to say goodbye to my friends. It was hard to say goodbye to the preschool where I was volunteering at. Goodbyes are hard. I was very independent in Los Angeles. I miss the amusement parks. I miss volunteering on Skid Row. I miss my friends.

When we got to North Carolina I had a very hard adjustment. I missed my family and my life back in Los Angeles, California. That Fall 2019 I joined the Special Olympics basketball team. I made several new friends on the team. We went down to Charlotte, NC to the state games. We came in second place. The game we played was really intense. It took me a while to get used to living in North Carolina. It was really hard to make friends. It still is hard to make friends.

When I got here I started doing puzzles. I really love doing puzzles. We found some really good restaurants. We went to the movies a lot. We had movie passes. We would go on fun hikes like Julian price in Blowing Rock. My mom and I started volunteering at the Cooperative Christian

Ministry in Hickory. We would work in the food pantry. We met some awesome people there.

It was hard adjusting to Hickory coming from Los Angeles. I was able to focus on the positive things about Hickory. I love Hickory. It is a great city to live in. I love living by the lake. I love our neighbors. I love swimming in the lake. I love our church Mountain View Baptist Church. I love my job at Chick Fil A. I love Adult Life.

Country life on the lake has had its ups and downs. Coming from the big city was a huge adjustment. We have been in Hickory for almost 5 years now. The time has flown by. We love lake life. I love walking in my neighborhood and talking to all my neighbors. I love listening to music while I walk. I feel much safer walking around my neighborhood than I did in LA. We just got our pool put in. After waiting for a few years we finally got our pool put in. We love it so much. We are excited to have friends and neighbors over to go swimming in it. My family is really excited! We have a lot of different wildlife here in our neighborhood. We have snakes, bunnies, birds, turtles, deer, and cats. The weather in NC heats up during the summer with strong humidity. It gets cold in the winter. Spring and Fall are my favorite time of year. Life is Good because God is So Good.

When we first moved here in August of 2019 our next door David Carpenter took us out on his boat several times. I would ride on his raft he had that was tied to the back of his boat. He would take us out on his jet ski. He was such an awesome neighbor. I enjoyed spending time with him. I remember one November I jumped off his dock wearing a wetsuit into the lake.

During the summer my family has lake time. We go out on the lake and go paddle boarding or kayaking. I love to go on our jet ski's. I love to jump off our dock and swim in the lake. We have a boat we enjoy going on during the summer. During the summer there are isolated thunderstorms. The lighting lights up the sky and it pours rain in sheets. I love watching the lightning at night because it lights up my room. I love to hear the thunder. During the summer my family loves going to concerts in Hickory. We went to a couple cover bands. Last year we went to a restaurant that you parked your boat on their dock and ate at their restaurant. Summers here are very hot and humid. Sometimes it is hard to go to Carowinds in the heat.

During our 5 years that we have lived here we have found several different trails and restaurants that we love. Our favorite hiking trail is Julian Price Loop in Blowing Rock. Blowing Rock is a beautiful town about an hour or so away from Hickory. We love eating at Mellow Mushroom after a good hike. We also love Woodland and River Bend that are closer to where we live. They are great hikes too, but these hikes take a while and can be hard at times. My family loves El Paso for Mexican food. We also love Longhorn steakhouse too. We tend to go back to the same restaurants multiple times. We love Jason's Deli. I love ordering their spaghetti. It is so good.

Another fun adventure we did while living in North Carolina is riding a mountain coaster. It was an awesome experience. It was really fun traveling out to find this mountain coaster and riding it. I remember visiting Pigeon Forge, Tennessee. It was an incredible town with so much fun things to do. They have a ride where I flip upside down several times. I went on it and loved it!! I love trying the different activities and seeing what there is out in this part of the world.

North Carolina sure has its challenges, but I am so grateful for the opportunities to embrace life out here. I miss life back in Los Angeles, but I am forever grateful for my life out here. It was a hard adjustment moving cross country but looking back it was worth it. I remember traveling by car all the way from Los Angeles to Hickory with 2 dogs Daisy and Noel at the time. It took us 3 in a half days on the road. We stopped at Chipotle a few times on the road. We made it to Hickory at the end of July of 2019. A lot has changed since then. I am grateful for the learning opportunities. God is So Good!! All the time God is Good!!

I love the weather in North Carolina. We have the four seasons. Spring is beautiful and the weather is really nice. Summer is hot and humid. Fall is cooler and the weather is perfect. Winter is cold and gloomy. I love during the Summer months watching the lightning light up my bedroom during the night. I love seeing the pouring rain and hearing the thunder.

I love seeing all the wildlife in North Carolina. We have so many different animals. My favorites are the deer and the bunnies. I love to see all the horses and cows and chickens. I have a huge heart for animals. I love them. It's so different coming from the big city to the country. I love it though despite its challenges.

I love my neighborhood. I have amazing neighbors. I love to walk around the neighborhood and listen to music. I love to say Hi and chat with the neighbors. We have social hours and a yearly BBQ gathering for our neighborhood.

The biggest question is How does my disability affect me at my job? This is a very hard question to answer. Sometimes my co-workers and managers have a hard time understanding me and my special needs. I had really good managers over the years for my jobs.

When I was younger I was in a program in high school called workability. It was a job program for students with disabilities. I took on several different little jobs. Jobs that lasted a few months. I learned how to wipe down tables, help customers, and sweep the floors at the different places I worked. I worked at El Tarasco, HomeGoods, Walgreens, and my school cafeteria. I enjoyed my jobs there.

Chapter 11: Work Life

One ordinary day in September of 2016 I really wanted to apply to my all-time favorite fast food restaurant Chipotle in El Segundo, California. I applied several different times and interviewed. I wasn't able to get the job. After trying so hard I decided to seek out help from different special needs job support services. The people came out to help me interview and I landed the job. I was beyond excited it was a dream come true. When I walked through their doors I was so happy to be part of such a great company. I was treated respectfully by my General Manager. She told me Andrew I don't want to set you up for failure. What she meant was that she didn't want me on the line during peak hours due to high levels of stress. I really wanted to help out on the line. She said I don't want to set you up to fail. They put me in the dining room. I helped clean tables, restock ice and utensils, sweep, mop, take out trash, etc. I was really good at this job. I spent about 2 in and half to 3 years there. When I got to my new town Hickory, North Carolina I live in now I transferred to the restaurant there. I was put on the line because it was a smaller less busy restaurant. At that time August 2019 I did a great job. I enjoyed the employees.

I remember when I worked for Chipotle they strived to be Top Performers. What is a Top Performer? It is a person who has the desire and ability to perform great work and in doing so it elevates them, their team, and the company. In life I strive everyday to be a top performer in whatever I do. In my job I especially desire to be a top performer.

One day in March I decided to rent an apartment. This was a huge deal for me and my mom. My mom and I are extremely close. March and April were the toughest months of my life. When I got to my apartment I noticed my health was declining and my job at Chipotle was as well. I asked myself why? The reason being was I was on the line for longer shifts and something was wrong with my mental health. It was fine for a period of time. Once Covid slowed down the restaurant got so much busier. Most of you know that I do not manage stress well. I know we all deal with stress, but when you come back to your new home and lay on the floor, waking up in the middle of the night chugging apple juice. Something isn't right. When you know something doesn't feel right inside your heart then something probably isn't right. I had stress from the medications on top of work related stress on me.

One day at work I needed to use the restroom. I asked two different employees and they told me no I need to stay on the line. I was mortified. If an employee needs to use the restroom at work they need to use the restroom and have a right to do so. One Day I asked my manager for extra help. Right after that I stood up for myself and told her I can't handle the line without help. Yes I still got a little help not much though. She then told me Andrew if you can't handle the work then Thursday June 3rd, 2021 is your last day. I was upset because that is not how you treat your employees especially ones that work their tail off. You must give at least 2 week notice. I still wanted to work for the company but I got let go. I still enjoyed my experience there and I was sad they let me go.

So why was I so upset on June 3rd 2021. On June 3rd 2021 I left one of all my all time favorite restaurants Chipotle. I was told I couldn't use the bathroom twice and that I was making people miserable. I could not believe what I was hearing. So let me make myself clear I show up on time and pick up extra shifts. I do what I am told. I treat the people around me with respect. My mom puts tips in their tip jar. One day after busy lunch peak hours I need to use the bathroom and I am told no twice by two different employees. What the!! That is absolutely no way to treat another employee. Especially one who works so hard and gets taken advantage of. Then I am told I am making the people around me miserable because I am struggling and asking for help. Then finally one day I ask for help and the manager pulls me aside then lets me go. That is seriously the most ugliest way to treat a hard working mentally disabled human being. I was glad they were honest with me though. I couldn't really keep up with the pace of the restaurant anymore. I enjoyed my experience there.

See friends When we ask for help there are people who are willing to help us out and people who do not. During my time there I enjoyed my job. I enjoyed serving guests with a smile in the restaurant. The first day I got frustrated on the line I asked for help and got let go. See when we stick up for ourselves there are consequences sometimes. Yes the General Manager cared about me and did the best she could to help me out. When my body was shutting down on me it is time for me to leave. I'm not sure how much of this was Bipolar related. I think most of it was bipolar related symptoms. In my heart I did not want to leave Chipotle. I was very devastated inside because that is one of my all time favorite places. Working there was a great experience overall. I learned so much about customer service and know how to work with co workers. It broke my heart that I got treated how I did but overall I had such a great experience at Chipotle. I made new friends. I got discounts on meals. It was a great experience till the end. The managers at Chipotle noticed I was struggling a lot so they let me go. I didn't get fired.

In 2021 when this was all taken place I got hired at one of my favorite fast food restaurants Chick Fil A. One day I walked in with my Chick Fil A sweatshirt on and asked if the dining room position is available. The general Manager said yes it is. I filled out an application right there and interviewed and got hired pretty fast. I was beyond excited. I started on May 7th 2021. I was beyond excited for my new job. I love the dining room position because I loved interacting with the guests. It is such a great job for me. I enjoy wiping tables and refreshing peoples drinks. I enjoy asking the guests how their meal is and if there is anything I can get for them.

I have always loved getting up in the morning and going to work. I loved when I lived in the apartment and I would walk to work. I remember in El Segundo I would walk to Chipotle and walk or take the bus home. Working is something I value a lot. I feel work is so important because you contribute to the real world. You get to bump elbows with the real world. I love going to work when I am scheduled to work.

I am so happy at Chick Fil A!!!! There are days when the restaurant can be slow. I love refilling people's drinks and cleaning the tables. My favorite part is asking the guests how is their meal? I enjoy seeing all the children having fun in the playground. I love eating Grilled nuggets with fries and BBQ sauce. I love drinking Dr. Pepper, sweet tea, root beer, and Cherry Coke.

On Sundays at church I love serving in Children's ministry. I enjoy helping out in Kidzone with the other leaders. I am able to either have my own group of children or sit with another leader and help out. It is so much fun. I help out every other week because I love going to the main service with my mom.

My Dream job is to get a job onboard a cruise ship. Ever since I was little I have loved cruising. I loved traveling to exotic locations around the world. I am considering this Fall to apply and see where it will take me. I may or may not get it, but I will pray and seek God's Will in all things. I have good experiences working in the restaurant industry.

I love the work that I do. It brings me so much joy to help people. I meet so many awesome people when I am working. Ever since I started in my school cafeteria back in high school I have learned so much in the field of hospitality. God has been so Good to me. He has been so faithful.

Back in 2013 I started volunteering at my church in their Awana program. I helped out with Awana Cubbies preschool for a couple years and then Awana Sparks kindergarten for a year or two. It was so much fun. In Awana the children recite their Bible Versus. It was really fun to help them learn them. Every week we would sit on the carpet and hear a Bible Story. There were excellent leaders that helped out too. I enjoyed every Wednesday evening taking the bus down to Journey of Faith and helping out. I even helped out at Vacation Bible School a couple of years. I enjoyed helping out the other leaders with snacks, games, and Bible Lessons.

in 2014 I helped out at a Vacation Bible School at someone's house. I showed up everyday ready to help and serve. The leader who was in charge said to me "get in there and help". I got so offended because that was the reason why I was there. I wanted to help out. I have a learning disability and have a hard time knowing what to do in situations. She really made me feel like crap. I do my best in every situation. I try to help as best I can.

In 2014 I started volunteering at St John's Preschool in El Segundo. I would go once or twice a week and help out in the different classrooms. I loved serving at the preschool. My favorite ages were the 3 and 4 year olds. They were so much fun to interact with. I loved watching the children as they played outside with their peers. I loved all the teachers and staff too. They welcomed me as a volunteer. That is where I started really enjoying working with children. I started studying Child Development at West Los Angeles College during that time.

In 2014 I got to serve with the middle school group at my church called Ignite. Michelle was the head leader and she was incredible. I learned so much for volunteering with them. I enjoyed Sunday mornings at 9:30am serving with them. I loved Michelle's messages and the powerful worship songs. I enjoyed going out into the community with them. We would help out in the community. We also went to Six Flags Magic Mountain a few times as well. The students were great. The volunteers were really nice as well.

In 2015 I started volunteering with School on Wheels. School on Wheels is an after school tutoring homeless children program for students kindergarten through 12th grade that meet on Skid Row. Skid Row is famous in Los Angeles for homelessness. Every week I would take the bus from El Segundo to Skid Row in Downtown Los Angeles. I would be paired with kindergarten and first grade students and help them with their homework. We would go on field trips too. We went to the California Science Center and the Aquarium of the Pacific. I helped watch the students as they had a great time.

The biggest thing I have learned about children that it is so important to always show up for them. Showing up and showing children that you care is the most important thing. The first is teaching them about Jesus Christ. Second is showing and caring for them. I have a huge heart for Children. My heart breaks for the children in the world today. I am so grateful for the opportunity to minister to children at my church and am so grateful that I got to help with preschoolers when I lived in Los Angeles. I miss working with preschoolers, but I enjoy working with kindergarten through 5th graders at my church.

I am so proud of your children. One of the greatest things I experience in this life is watching your children grow up. I understand how hard this life is. If is hard for me I can only imagine how hard it must be for children. I am forever grateful for the experiences I have had serving in Children's ministry and I am so glad I get to continue serving in Children's ministry.

Chapter 12: 2021

2021 was by far the hardest year in North Carolina. In 2020 I got put on anti-depressant medications for what I was going through. I was experiencing depression and harmful thoughts. In February of 2021 I got put on a strong dose of Fluoxetine 40mg. It made my body feel out of control.

In March of 2021 I wanted to move into my own apartment. In April my mom and stepdad Dave helped me move into my new apartment. I signed a 6month lease. The first month was so hard because I was waking up in the middle of the night and chugging apple juice. I was working at Chipotle at the time. I was struggling at work because Covid had ended and the restaurant was much busier. One day in May I needed extra help and they let me go because I wasn't able to keep up with the job. I had a couple mental breakdowns while at work. They weren't extreme but still were noticeable.

One ordinary day in April I was walking to church from my apartment. I crossed the street over to a church called New Jerusalem I wanted to try. About half way or so into the service a policeman asks me to come outside. I was very confused, but I did what he told me. He was concerned because I was walking down the side of the road. He was very nice. I didn't get arrested or anything like that, but I was concerned. I was very respectful. In life we will interact with police officers.

It is extremely important to treat them with respect. My mom has always taught me and my sister to respect the police and authority.

Hickory doesn't have much sidewalks so I had to walk to church or take a van from the apartment. My apartment was named the Legends. I loved it very much, but was missing home a lot. I walked down Startown Road to Discovery Church. Most of the time I would take the church van to church so I didn't have to walk. I was able to walk to New Life Fellowship which was closer than Discovery Church.

I loved having my own apartment. I lived in a one bedroom one bathroom apartment in Hickory near my work. I enjoyed the amenities. I enjoyed the pool. I enjoyed the fitness center and the basketball court. I enjoyed doing laundry there. I loved being a part of Discovery Church and New Life Fellowship church. I loved Discovery's Wednesday night prayer and worship service. I loved the pastor and their sermons at both the churches I attended. I enjoyed the young adult group at Discovery Church.

In May I got hired at my favorite restaurant Chick Fil A. I started on May 7th, 2021. I was so happy to get a new job while living close by at the apartment. I remember my first day on the job I started in the dining room. I loved cleaning tables and interacting with the guests. I loved refreshing people's drinks.

June 3rd, 2021 was my last day at Chipotle. I was very sad to leave the company but proud of spending 4 in a half years with the company.

That weekend my family went up to Portland Maine for the weekend to celebrate my Grandpa's birthday. My mom noticed something really off with my mental health. I was acting really weird. I had another mental breakdown. It was nice seeing my cousins and aunt and uncle and spending time with my grandpa.

On Monday June 7th my mom took me to the hospital. I got admitted. I was there for four in a half days. I got diagnosed with Bipolar. It was a really scary time for me and my family. I got taken off all the anti-depressant medication I was on. I had great medical care. They took good care of me.

After the hospital I returned to work and slowly recovered. I still felt off and over the summer I became very depressed. Bipolar is a mental illness where you experience mania and depression episodes. In August my mom and I decided I should see a psychiatrist. I was able to get in and see one. He put me on lithium. A few days later I felt really weird. I took myself off of it. I was fine for a few months. Never take yourself off any medication without consulting your doctor or health care provider first.

In August I moved back home. Even though I missed my family at home, I missed my independence while living at the apartment. Never make big decisions when you are unstable.

In August my mom took me on a trip up to Cedar Point in Sandusky, Ohio. I had an amazing time. I spent two days at the park. On Friday I got on everything I wanted to. The lines were short. I loved Steel Vengeance and Maverick. I also loved Millennium Force as well. I met a wonderful person named Tammy. She was so nice. She didn't like the roller coasters like I did tough. The next day I went back to the park and went on the coasters again. I had such a fun time. In 2022 I went back to the park and I got on some more coasters. It was more busy then when I went the year before. I met Tammy's Sister named Tracy. She was really nice too. We rode Gemini together. In 2022 my mom took me to the

Mall of America. They had some really fun roller coasters in the mall. It was really neat.

In February of 2022 I went on a big trip to Antarctica with my mom and grandpa. I noticed I was having a very hard time sleeping. When I got home I experienced another manic episode. I went back to the hospital and they got in touch with my psychiatrist. He told me to take the lithium and Abilify. I got back on it and within a few days I was feeling a lot better. I was so glad to have a psychiatrist. It is really helpful to have someone to talk to and help me with my medications.

In May of 2022 I flew back to Los Angeles and stayed with my family for about a month. I enjoyed it. I got to see my friends Ben and Matt. I got to visit the preschool that I volunteered at. I got to ride buses around town. I stayed with Matt Clebowicz for a few days at his apartment out in the valley. We went to Six Flags Magic Mountain. I miss it there.

In September of 2022 I joined Special Olympics Tennis. It was so much fun going to practice. I met a special friend named Heather Taliaferro. We hung out and went out to eat with our families. We enjoyed the tennis season. I got to participate in the championship games in Charlotte. I tied first place in my division. Tennis was really fun. It was my first time ever playing tennis. I feel I did a great job at the sport. It is great connecting with Heather and her family. I enjoy spending time with them. They are great people.

Chapter 13: Bipolar and Medication

One ordinary day in October of 2020 I was experiencing some harmful thoughts. I decided it was time to seek medical help. My mom and I thought I should see a counselor. I signed up to meet with a counselor in Hickory to discuss what I was feeling. My doctor put me on anti-depressant medication. Slowly I started feeling better but the symptoms were still there.

After a few months of medication and counseling I got put on a high dose of fluoxetine 40mg. I was noticing really weird things happening to my body. I was waking up in the middle of the night. I was having intense feelings inside. I was doing really weird things that I was not used to doing before. I was saying bizarre things. Both my counselor and doctor didn't know what was going on.

I was experiencing a weird symptom where I would inappropriately laugh. I was experiencing this for several years where sometimes my laughing would be inappropriate and be out of control. Like during the middle of prayer I would burst out laughing. Ever since I started on medication that has calmed down tremendously. I am so glad that has settled down. It was really embarrassing.

On June 7th, 2021 My mom took me into the emergency room at the hospital. I got admitted to the hospital and was there for four in a half days. At the hospital I got evaluated and was diagnosed with Bipolar. It was a relief because they got to the root of the problem. I was so thankful for such great care at the hospital. The anti depressant medication I was on was causing the Bipolar to spark. So that is why my body was doing really weird things.

After the hospital I was still living at the apartment. During the summer of 2021 I became very depressed. I went back to work and was having a hard time recovering. In August I moved back home and my mom took me to a physchiatrist. He put me on lithium. I took it for a few days and then I felt really weird. I was ok till February of 2022. I went on a big trip. On the trip I noticed I wasn't sleeping well. I was experiencing another manic episode. We went back to the hospital and they contacted my physchiatrist. He said I need to stay on lithium and he also prescribed me abilify. After a few days I was feeling so much better.

Several months later I felt another little episode came on but I caught it right away before it got worse. How do I know I am about to experience another episode? The biggest symptom is sleep. When I wake up in the early morning hours and can't get back to sleep. When I talk really fast and talk a lot. When I feel I am about to have a mental breakdown at work or at home. It is time to seek medical help. I am so glad I sought help when I did. I really believe if I hadn't sought help I would be in big trouble. Bipolar is a serious mental illness that should be taken seriously. Bipolar is a mood disorder where you experience high mania and low depression episodes. During Mania I have very very high energy and lots of it and feel I won't be able to sleep. I also feel very irritable. I feel very impulsive too. If you feel any of these symptoms I strongly recommend contacting your doctor right away or go to the hospital. Never stop taking medication without first talking to your doctor first. You can have a bad relapse if you abruptly stop your medication.

I am forever grateful for the support of my family over the years. This has not been an easy road. Having a mental illness is a serious thing. It must be hard for any parent to find out their children are mentally ill. I probably got Bipolar when I was in high school. I am grateful for excellent doctors and an excellent physchiatrist from the hospital. I feel so much better right now. Even though I still have Bipolar It is easily controlled. I am now able to tell when I am about to have a breakdown or an episode.

In the beginning I had no idea about Bipolar. My doctor, counselor, and my family had no idea about my Bipolar. I was very scared about what was happening to me. That is why it is so important if you are experiencing symptoms to contact your health care provider right away. If you feel something is weird and doesn't feel right it is time to seek medical help. Before doctors and anyone can help you, you first have to doctor yourself. If I knew I had Bipolar back in early 2021 I would have completely done things differently. The anti-depressant meds made my symptoms really worse, but I am glad I went to the hospital to get checked out. Once I got the diagnosis things started to really make sense.

Today I am able to manage my symptoms. I feel when I am starting to get manic. I know when I am having a mental breakdown. Bipolar is a scary thing and I am so glad I have the weapons to battle it. God is forever Faithful. He will constantly take care of me and he brought me through the most darkest days of my life back in 2021. No one will understand your story until they experience the same things for themselves.

14 |

Chapter 14: 2023

2023 was a really challenging year in so many way. In March my family adopted a bloodhound girl. Her name is Bonnie. The place that we adopted her from told us she was 3 years old, but it turns out she is only about a year old. She is a handful of a dog. She went to doggie boot camp in April to get trained. She is now a better dog, but still very puppy like. We love her very much. I enjoy playing with Bonnie. She can be very fistey. She is still learning a lot. I love going on her daily walk with my mom. I love when she climbs up into my lap even though she is a big dog. Bonnie is about 2 years old now.

On March 8th my mom and I got into a scary car accident. We were driving down the road heading to have lunch with friends. Out of now where there was a truck flipping at full speed in the air heading straight for our car and he crashed right into the front of our car. My mom screamed Andrew are you ok!!! We both walked out with only some cuts, blood, and scars. It was the scariest accident of my life. Back in November of 2015 I was crossing the street near my house and I got hit by a car. I had a broken Tibia bone. I was in 3 different leg casts, crutches, and a knee scooter. I am always amazed at God's protection. I am forever grateful I walked out of those car accidents. Even If I have died I know where I am going when I die. I was really scared when the car accidents happened.

Back in 2015 I was walking to the bus stop. Out of nowhere I got hit by a car. I fell down to the ground and broke my left tibia bone. I was in 3 different casts. One upper thigh cast and two lower leg casts. I used crutches and a knee scooter. It was a really scary time. It was like a 12 week healing process. I had physical therapy to help strengthen my leg. I am constantly reminded of God's protection and his constant healing. I am forever grateful for those opportunities because it was an opportunity to strengthen my faith.

In early 2023 a very sad friendship ended. I was very sad that this happened and happened the way it did. We were just heartbroken. To this day I am still processing and grieving the friendship loss. We should never handle these type of situations over the phone. My mom and I are still processing the situation and we can not believe what happened. We have tried so hard to be kind and reach out to them. I have learned that when a person shows you their true colors believe them. In other words when people treat you badly multiple times quit being friends with them. I don't mean be mean to them. I am saying if you feel mistreated it is best to find a new friendship. Showing Character is extremely important. What is Character? Character is traits of a person. It is how you treat people. It is how a person behaves. Trust your Instincts. If something doesn't feel right then something probably isn't right. Even though I am still hurting about the friendship I am learning that it is just meant to be and he wasn't a good friend at all. That is hard to say but that is the truth. My mom would always say "bad things happen because good people stand around and do nothing" If no one corrects the behavior it keeps getting worse and worse till nobody will do anything about it and no changes will take place. I believe the reason why we are in the mess we are in today is because no one wants to correct bad behavior anymore so as a result we have poor behaved children, poor parenting, people not wanting to work, students out of control in the classroom. If we were to stand up for what is right and teach people how to behave I think the problems wouldn't be as bad as it is now.

As a Christian I could not believe how I was treated by another Christian. As Christians we are commanded to love and forgive. The only way people will know we are Christians is by how we treat and love each other. I believe that reading the Bible is important and going to church is important, but the most important thing is how we treat the people all around us. I was heartbroken when my friend and his mom spat in our faces but I learned a very valuable lesson from it.

What does it mean to be Demon-Possesed? I believe Satan is alive and everywhere today. If it is not of God it is of Satan. I believe he is deceiving people left and right. He wants to bring as many people to Hell with him as he can. Satan is the great deceiver. He comes to steal, kill, and destroy. He sneaks into people's lives and lies to them. He whispers things in peoples ears and people listen to him and are deceived. Satan knows his days are short so he is trying to deceive as many people as he can.

Growing up I made friends and it turns out there weren't my friends at all. I would refer to them as Fantasy friends. I had a lot of those in my lifetime. I was nice and kind to them, but a lot of them didn't understand my disability. Some of those people have disabilities which is crazy to me how we can have similar learning challenges and still not get along.

So who is a friend? Friends have your back. Friends don't hurt you or your family. Friends are people who care about you. Friends tell you the truth even though you may not want to hear it. I remember in middle school in the school psychologist's room he had a poster and it said "the only way to have a friend is to be a friend" If you are not a friend to someone then chances are you will likely have a hard time making friends. Friends are always with you through hard times. When I was experiencing difficult seasons in my life I knew who really cared about me and who didn't. A friend cries when you cry and laughs when you laugh. A friend does not talk about you behind your back. A friend stands beside you through thick and thin good and bad times. It is hard work making friends. For me it is very hard because of my disability. I am grateful for my friends.

In September my mom took me on an amazing trip to the 5 Stans. Uzbekistan, Turkmenistan, Kazakhstan, Tajikistan and Kyrgyzstan. I had an amazing time with my mom. We saw some awesome countries. We had 8 different guides. We took 15 different flights. We met my sister down in Nepal and Bhutan at the end of the trip. We all had a great trip and made so many amazing memories.

For my 30th birthday I wanted to try skydiving. There is a place about an hour or so away from where I live. I always loved roller coasters growing up. About a year or so ago I found a website about skydiving. I wanted to try it out. My mom said yes so on November 16th 2023 my mom took me down to the Skydiving center. I signed a waiver and met my guide. My guide is named Kyle. He was amazing. I got all harnessed up and headed over to the airplane. I went up 13,000 thousand feet. Both of us jumped out of the airplane and I screamed. It was really scary during freefall. I went 120mph for 40-45 seconds. The parachute ride was really fun too. It was like a 5-7 minute ride down to Earth. It was a successful jump. I would do it again.

2023 was a very challenging year in ways. In other ways it was a great year. I learned a lot and grew in my faith. I pray that 2024 and beyond are great too. I pray I grow even deeper in my faith. Thank you all for joining me on this wild journey. I am forever grateful for my family and friends who have joined me on my journey. You are all amazing!!! I love you all!!! I wish you all a happy and healthy 2024 and beyond!!!

Chapter 15: Family Life

I have a loving family. I have an amazing mom who took really good care of me and my sister. I absolutely adore my mom. She was a single mom who raised me and my sister Alison. She was a middle school special education basic skills teacher who taught for 17 years. She saw me through my challenging years of childhood and young adulthood. She would take us out to eat and buy us school clothes. She took me and my sister to church from the time we were infants. My mom taught me and my sister all about Jesus Christ and how to trust in him as my personal Lord and Savior. I became a Christian in middle school. My mom took me and my sister to Disneyland when we were younger. We would go on Fridays after school. She took me and my cousins to Six Flags Magic Mountain growing up. I remember going on the roller coasters with my cousins Connor and Collin. We rode rides like Revolution and Psyclone. We would ride Colossus too. I remember my mom took our really great friends The Morgans to Six Flags Magic Mountain. Deborah Morgan and my mom were great friends growing up. They are still great friends today. We all went to Six Flags Magic Mountain on a day in middle school and I rode Viper for the first time with Melissa Morgan. Viper is the 7 loops roller coaster at Six Flags Magic Mountain. It became my favorite roller coaster at Six Flags Magic Mountain.

My biological dad helped take care of me too. My mom got divorced when I was very little. I don't really remember it because I was so little. I loved going over to my dad's house and spending time with him. He would take me to carnivals and amusement parks when I was younger. I miss my dad so much since I have moved to North Carolina. I also miss Tayna Dad's Fiance. I miss eating at their house and having Fritto Misto for dinner. I enjoy flying out to visit them in California. In North Carolina a year or so ago I started a workout session with my dad on video chat. I started at 5 pounds then went up to 8 pounds. I was doing 10 pounds for a while. I am enjoying it. Now I do it on my own during the week. I love my family from my dad's side. Aunt Debbie, Aunt Robin, and Aunt Amy are awesome people who I really miss. I can still see them in California for a visit.

My family had several dogs growing up. Roxy we adopted as a puppy. We adopted her in 2001. She was a very nervous doggie. She was very loyal. She was a great dog. In 2002 we adopted Rusty. Rusty was a very funny dog. She was very dumb. She was a great doggie too. In 2009 we adopted our German Shepherd purebread named Max. We had him for 4 years. We had Rusty for 10 years and Roxy for 17 years. In 2015 we adopted our first bloodhound lab named Bruiser. Bruiser was a special boy. He was such a great dog. in 2017 we adopted another bloodhound named Daisy. She was a special girl too. She was a foodie. Bruiser we had for 2 years and Daisy we had for 5 years. Today we have Bonnie our bloodhound. She is just about 2 years old. She keeps my family on our toes. She is wild. She is a love though. We love our dogs. Several dogs have come and gone but they are remain in our hearts forever.

My Grandparents Arnold and Shirley Durtschi were some of the most special people in my life. My grandma was a such a special lady. Growing up we would always go over to their house and make lunch or dinner. We would go there every Christmas morning and do gifts and sometimes stockings. Every Sunday at church I would sit next to my Grandma and Grandpa in the big service. After church we would all go out to lunch at California Pizza Kitchen or other restaurants around the South Bay. We went to Journey of Faith formerly called Community

Baptist Church in Manhattan Beach, CA. My grandma Shirley passed away in April of 2018. She is dearly missed and she was deeply loved by so many. She taught me and my family many things. She loved church. She loved America. She dearly loved her family. My Grandpa is almost 90. He is still living with us today. I love spending quality time with him. We love watching Wheel of Fortune together and eating at Captain Galley and Wendy's He loves his family very much. He is enjoying North Carolina. We are taking my Grandpa on a 7 day Great Lakes cruise onboard the Viking Expedition ship for his 90th birthday. We had an amazing time on the 7 day Great Lakes Cruise. Grandpa really enjoyed himself on the cruise. It was a great time!!

I have the most amazing sister. Her name is Alison. Alison and I have always gotten along. There were seasons where we argued with each other, but that is normal in families. We would love to go out to eat with my mom to Mongolian BBQ. We loved each other dearly. She has been a constant support with me over the years as I went through challenging times at school. Even at home too. We loved going to Disney's California Adventure and riding California Screamin. We would go to Six Flags Fright Fest at Six Flags Magic Mountain. We would go for Halloween and enjoy all the scary haunted mazes. My mom taught Alison and I how to trust in Jesus Christ as our personal Lord and Savior. Alison became a Christian at a young age like me.

I would always love to spend time with my cousins Connor and Collin OBryan. We would go to amusement parks and have sleep overs. We would enjoy video games and play basketball together. We all would go out to eat. We would go to Vinces Spaghetti house in Torrance. That was my all-time favorite restaurant to go to growing up. We would all go to the movies and have lunch or dinner at Sammy's Woodfired Pizza. They would all join us for Christmas morning at my Grandparents house. We would eat waffles and then open gifts. Our favorite place to eat growing up is Cheesecake Factory. We would sit outside a lot on their patio and watch everyone go by. We would enjoy our meal together as a family. I miss those days. Having lunch with my entire family are things I will cherish for the rest of my life. I miss my cousins, but I am so glad I can still message them and talk to them on the phone. I get to to see them from time to time.

Matt, and Sean have been great friends over the years. Matt and Sean are great stepbrothers. I enjoyed growing up with them and spending time with them. We would all go on trips and have so much fun. We would be silly and laugh. I enjoy visiting them and spending time with them. Dave has been a constant support over the years. I love seeing him love my mom. That is really special. I enjoy visiting Cher Matt and Sean's mom. She has been a loving support over the years ever since I was little. I would go over to Cher's house when I was little and we would all play video games and eat delicious meals. We would also go to the movies too. I remember Cher took us karaoking and I sang Puff The Magic Dragon. To this day I enjoy listening to that song. I am forever grateful for Cher and her loving and generous heart. She did a lot for me and my sister growing up and I am so grateful.

Family is extremely important to me. I love spending time with my family. For me I feel it is the second most important thing. First is a personal relationship with Jesus Christ.

We had a family tradition where every year when I was younger my cousins and grandparents would come over and we would have Chili. We would make popcorn balls and then walk down to Candy Cane Lane in El Segundo. I really enjoyed this tradition with my family. It was great to spend time together. I love spending time with my cousins. We would laugh and have fun.

Chapter 16: From Roller Coasters To Skydiving

When I was little I would always love to go to Carnivals. I would go with my dad. I would love to go to Disneyland with my family too. I would love to ride Space Mountain and Big Thunder Mountain. Growing up I loved roller coasters and carnivals.

Growing up me and my sister and our friends would love to visit Six Flags Fright Fest. Six Flags Magic Mountain put on an incredible Halloween scary event every year. They would have scary haunted mazes. My mom would take us after school several years. It was so much fun. I remember enjoying all the rides before it was time for the mazes. I remember the log ride was turned into a maze type attraction.

Growing up I would always love to go to Six Flags Magic Mountain. I would love to ride Viper and Scream. Those were my two favorite rides. When I was barely 48inches tall I went on Gold Rusher. Magic Mountain's first roller coaster. I was so brave to go on a roller coaster when I was that young. As I got older I went on rides like Colossus, Ninja, and Freefall. They had a really fun log ride too. I remember I went with my family for my 12th birthday. Matt and I went on Riddler's Revenge. As it started up the hill the ride came to a halt. My restraint wasn't buckled in properly. I was really concerned but I really enjoyed the ride. Over the years I rode many other roller coasters in the park.

In 2012 they added a huge freefall drop tower ride off the structure of one of their roller coasters. Drop of Doom took riders up 400 feet and dropped them at 85mph in 5 seconds straight down. I would enjoy visiting the park with family and friends. In 2013 I took the bus for the first time to the park. I took several trains and buses to get there. The trip took over 3 hours each way. I took the Greenline to the Blue Line to the Red Line train to North Hollywood. From there I took the 757 Noho bus to McBean Transit center from there I took the 3 or 7 to Six Flags Magic Mountain. I would do this several times. I would use my bus pass and hop on the different trains and buses. My friend from UCLA Matt Clebowicz would enjoy going to the park so we took the bus several times. Six Flags Magic Mountain holds a special place in my heart as my favorite amusement park roller coaster capital. I have so many fond memories of the park from the time I was a young child till the time I took public transportation to the park as an adult.

Growing up my grandparents would take the family to Knott's Berry Farm. I remember riding Ghost rider and Montezuma's Revenge when I was younger. I loved Knott's Berry Farm. They have amazing roller coasters there. My top favorites are Ghostrider, Silver Bullet, and Hangtime. Back in 2015 I started taking the bus and train from El Segundo the park. I took the Greenline and the 460 bus. I remember I met up with a friend from India we made on our trip there. She was with a group of students. We rode Hangtime together. It was really fun. I have visited Knott's Berry Farm several times in my lifetime and have enjoyed each and every moment there. It was fun because the rides I went on as a child I went on again as an adult and still really enjoyed them.

Over the years my mom would buy us Six Flags passes. They were good at any of the Six Flags across the country. When we traveled my mom would take us to several of the different parks around the country. My Favorite was Six Flags Over Texas and Six Flags Great Adventure. I had so much fun visiting the different parks and going on all the roller coasters. I am forever grateful for the lasting memories that were made at these different parks.

In 2010 my mom took me and my sister to Six Flags Great Adventure in New Jersey. At Six Flags Great Adventure they have the worlds tallest and fastest roller coaster when it opened in 2005. It is called Kingda Ka. When we woke up that morning it was pouring rain. My mom said kids I don't know should we try? We said yes lets do it. We got in our car and drove to the park. When the park opened we ran straight for Kingda Ka. We got in line and got onto it. It was the most intense roller coaster I have ever ridden. It launches from 0-128mph in 3.5 seconds and climbs 456 feet into the air. After Kingda ka I went on several different roller coasters in the park before the rain hit. I remember I went on a kid coaster and got drenched from the rain. I had my Cherry Chocolate phone I got for my 8th grade graduation in my pocket. It got soaked and completely ruined. I was phoneless for the remainder of that trip. I survived though. Lol.

When I got to North Carolina I got to to to go to Carowinds. At Carowinds they have the most thrilling roller coasters. My all time favorite is Fury 325. It is the tallest and fastest Giga coaster in the USA. I love Copperhead Strike as well. It is such a unique ride. Carowinds is in Charlotte, North Carolina.

About a year or so ago I found an awesome skydiving website. The skydiving facility is near where I live now. I asked my mom if I could skydive for my 30th birthday. She said yes you can. I was beyond excited. I was going to jump out of an airplane for the first time. I was really scared to do this. I went a week early before my birthday because of weather conditions. On November 16th my mom drove me down to the drop zone and I got ready. I put my harness on and headed over to the plane. It went up to 13,000 feet. When the door opened a rush of fresh air came through the plane. I was third in line to jump with Kyle.

It was my turn and we both jumped out together. It was extremely scary during freefall. I was going 120mph for 40-45 seconds. Freefall was really fun and really scary. The parachute was really fun too. I loved the scenery on the way down. The landing was smooth. I lifted my legs and slid in on my bottom. It was a successful first jump. I would for sure jump again. Growing up I never would have thought of skydiving. I loved roller coasters. I love the thrill of roller coasters. One day for my 30th birthday I decided to go skydiving. I am so glad I made the choice. It was an incredible experience.

17

Chapter 17: Wrap Up

Wow!! I can't believe 30 years has gone by. I remember when I was a child and that felt like it was yesterday. I loved going to amusement parks. I loved school for the most part. I grew stronger in my faith in Jesus Christ.

In conclusion as we all move into the new year let me remind you that even though this life is hard never give up. Always have a positive attitude. Always have a heart wide open. There are so many things to be thankful for. I know deep down that life is hard. I know we are facing spiritual warfare all around us. I know Jesus Christ is coming again real soon. I believe we are living in the last days. The Bible is real. Jesus Christ is Real.

2018, 2019, 2021, and 2023 were some of the most challenging years I have lived. From Jenna, to Moving across the country, to Moving into a new apartment, the list goes on and on. What I have learned is that when trials and tribulations come my faith is made stronger. I become a stronger Christian when I face troubles. God's power is made perfect in weakness. The Bible Says in this life you will face tribulation troubles. God does not promise us an easy life. He does promise he is always with us constantly. I will rejoice in the lord and I will say it again I will rejoice. In every circumstance I will trust Jesus Christ.

2024 has been a crazy year so far. I like Adult Life. I am making a lot of friends such as Glenn, Elizabeth, Lauren, Cole, Amanda, Heather and many more. My family is putting in a swimming pool and a dog run. We are upgrading our backyard. We are adding an outside kitchen. We are very excited. There are a lot of exciting things coming up. I am excited to see my childhood friend Ian in the Fall. I am grateful everyday for the blessings and the challenges. I am enjoying my job at Chick Fil A. I love my co-workers. I am so grateful for my job there.

I want to end with these questions. What legacy do you want to live for your children? Grandchildren? Great Grandchildren?

What legacy do you want to leave behind when you die? One day I am not going to be here. I want people to know how much I love and care about them. I want children to know that I care about them too. I want to live my best possible life here on earth. I want to live a Radical Relentless Christian life For Jesus Christ. I have very few regrets, I am forever grateful for this life. Even though life is hard and filled with learning challenges I am grateful for each and everyone of them. I have become a stronger person because of them.

This life its a race. I will run this relentless race for Jesus Christ to the finish line. One day I will cross the finish line and step foot into eternity. I will do my best here on earth. I will press on. I will fight the good fight. I don't know when that day will be, but I know it will be soon.

Everyday I am forever grateful for my journey called Life. Life has its up and downs. Life has its wild and crazy storms. Life has its challenges. Life has taught me so much. I am grateful for my family who have been by my side since I was born. I don't know what tomorrow holds, but I know who holds tomorrow. Everyday I am forever grateful in my heart. I live life with an attitude of gratitude. Life is far from easy. When I became a Christian several years ago I knew that life wasn't going to be easy. I remember a book I read several times as a child. I remember they had a saying in the book that said you can't go over it. You can't go under it. You have to go through it. That is the same as this journey called life. I can't escape the storms. I can't escape the sadness. I can't escape sin. I need to go through it. I go through it with a can do attitude. Life is a precious gift that God has given to me. Everyday is a gift. My story is a testimony to others. So what is your story? I am happy to listen and encourage you all on your journey. Thank you for all encouraging me on mine. You mean so much to me.

Thank you so much for joining me on my journey in this life. My life has not been an easy road, but my life is a testimony to others. Life has been such a blessing and a miracle. From the time I was little I had no idea what I would face growing up. Thank you to all my family and friends who have been there for me in my life. Life is better with friends and family around. I want to Thank and praise Jesus Christ who constantly is there for me in my times of growing up and today. I can't believe it is 2024. These years have gone by so fast. I can't believe I am 30 years old. The years fly by. I am so excited to see what God has in store for 2024 and Beyond!!!

My prayer for 2024 and beyond is. Dear Jesus I thank you for everything you have done for me in my life. I pray for a great year ahead. I pray I make new friends. I pray for all the children in this world. I pray you wrap your arms around them. I pray you comfort them with your love. I pray they come into a personal relationship with you. I thank you for letting me minister to them in their life at church. I pray as we face another election this year that you show us how to vote. You are always in control. I believe whatever happens it is in your will. I pray for Salvation for those who don't believe in you. I pray people come to know Jesus Christ as their Lord and Savior. I pray you take away my past hurts and heal my wounds. I thank you for a good year. I pray for my health that it can continue to be good. I thank you for healing me from my Bipolar even though I still have it. It is not as bad as it was it. I pray all these things in Jesus Name Amen!!!

Hello. My name is Andrew Mezen. I have been writing books for many years now. I enjoy it. This is my first every Chapter book. This book was fun to write. I hope you all enjoyed it. Thank you for supporting me and my writing.